Understanding
Applied Strategic Planning:
A Manager's Guide

J. William Pfeiffer,
Leonard D. Goodstein,
Timothy M. Nolan

San Diego ▪ Toronto
Amsterdam ▪ Sydney

ISBN: 0-88390-183-8
Library of Congress Catalog Card Number 85-50083

Printed in the United States of America

Table of Contents

Understanding Applied Strategic Planning:

A Manager's Guide

J. William Pfeiffer, Leonard D. Goodstein, and Timothy M. Nolan

Most organizations do some type of long-range or strategic planning, and the formal strategic planning process has been used for over thirty years. However, our experience as managers in and as consultants to a variety of organizations has convinced us that most strategic planning processes are poorly conceptualized and poorly executed; the strategic plan rarely impacts the day-to-day decisions made in the organization. To be successful, a strategic planning process should provide the criteria for making organizational decisions at all levels and should provide a template against which all such decisions can be evaluated.

When the managers of an organization are asked about its strategic plan, they frequently look pained or embarrassed and begin to search through their files to find the plan, which obviously is nonfunctional. All too often, strategic planning is seen as a top-level or staff exercise that has little to do with the actual running of the organization. In such cases, the majority of the managers—who make and implement decisions on a daily basis—are neither involved in the strategic planning process nor aware of the basic assumptions behind or operational implications of the strategic plan. In many cases, it is not too far-fetched to question whether a true strategic plan even exists.

A Definition of Strategic Planning

Strategic planning is the process by which the guiding members of an organization envision its future and develop the necessary procedures and operations to achieve that future. This vision of the future state of the organization provides both the direction in which the organization should move and the energy to begin that move. The envisioning process is very different from long-range planning—the simple extrapolation of statistical trends or forecasts—and it is more than attempting to anticipate the future and prepare accordingly. Envisioning involves a belief that aspects of the future can be influenced and changed by what one does now. Properly implemented, the strategic planning process presented here can help your organization to do more than *plan* for the future; it can help the organization to *create* its future.

Strategic planning is, however, more than just an envisioning process. It requires the setting of clear goals and objectives and the attainment of those goals and objectives within specified periods of time in order to reach the planned future state. Thus, targets must be developed within the context of the desired future state and must be realistic, objective, and attainable. The goals and objectives developed within the strategic planning process should provide the managers in the organization with a set of core priorities and guidelines for virtually all day-to-day managerial decisions.

This new model of strategic planning focuses on the *process* of planning, not the plan that is produced. Although documents delineating mission statements, strategic goals, functional objectives, and so on do emerge from the planning process, it is the process of self-examination, the confrontation of difficult choices, and the establishment of priorities that characterize successful strategic planning. Documents too often are merely filed away until revisions are mandated by some external force.

Strategic planning also is a reiterative process. Strategic planning and strategic management—the day-to-day implementation of the strategic plan—are the most important, never-ending tasks of all managers and especially those in top management. Once a strategic planning cycle is completed, the managers' task is to ensure its implementation and then to plan when to begin the next planning cycle. The future, by definition, always faces us; thus, organizations and the people who run them always must be in the simultaneous processes of planning and implementing plans.

A New Strategic Planning Model

This new model of strategic planning is based on existing models but differs in content, emphasis, and process. This model is especially useful for medium-sized and small organizations and is as useful for nonprofit organizations as it is for business and industrial organizations. The use of this model in your organization's strategic planning will provide both new direction and new energy to the organization. The model differs from others in its continual concern with application and implementation, not only after its completion but at every step along the way. Hence the title "Applied Strategic Planning Model." This booklet will highlight the process and the role of the planning team in regard to the rest of the organization. Further detail can be found in Pfeiffer, Goodstein, and Nolan (1986).

THE APPLIED STRATEGIC PLANNING MODEL

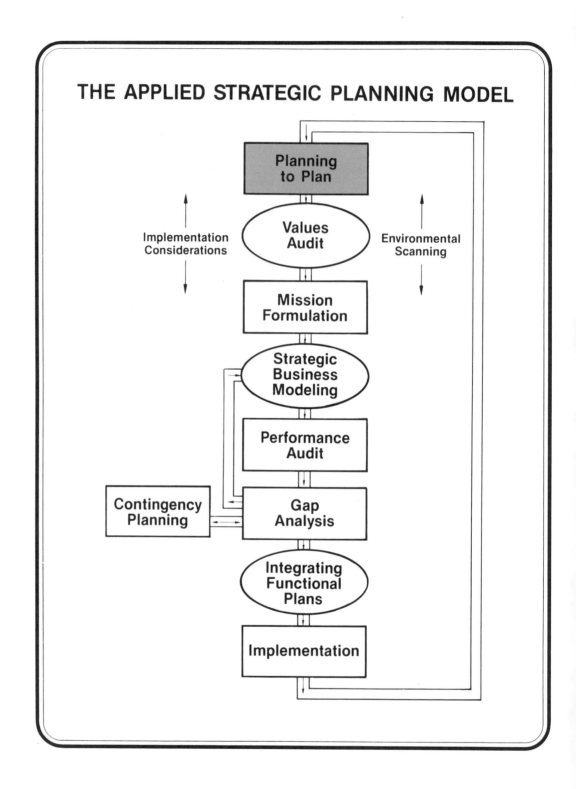

Phase One:
Planning To Plan

During the prework of the strategic planning process, your organization's top management—those people who are responsible for making key decisions—will be answering a host of questions and making a number of decisions, all of which are critically important to the eventual success or failure of the entire planning process. The questions include: How much commitment is there to the planning process? Who should be involved? How long will it take? What do we need to know in order to plan successfully? Who should develop the data? Planning to plan includes developing the answers to these questions and making these decisions prior to the initiation of any actual planning process. It is critically important not to rush into the process without clarifying various expectations, considering who will and who will not be involved, and so on. These issues must be resolved before the decision to plan can be made.

Commitment

The first step in planning to plan is to make certain that there is organizational commitment to the process—that the key people in the organization, especially the chief executive officer (CEO), see the planning process as important and are willing to invest time and effort in the process in a way that is visible to the rest of the organization. Steiner (1979) defines the CEO as the person or persons with the authority to manage the organization. Steiner (p. 80) points out that the CEO can be the president, the president and the executive vice president, or some other combination of individuals; in the case of a division of an organization, this authority can be exercised by a divisional manager or the like. What is critical is that this authority must be involved in the planning process in a highly visible way to signify commitment.

Identification of Planning Team

Once commitment from the chief executive officer is secured, the next concern is to identify the planning team. The CEO should be involved, especially in the early stages, as should other key people in the organization—those people who can represent the various functional aspects of the organization such as manufacturing, marketing, research, finance, and so on. During the initial phases of the planning process, those people *responsible* for functional units—usually at the vice presidential level—should be involved. The model presented here requires top-management involvement on a continuous basis; although it has been suggested elsewhere that the planning process be assigned to a staff group, we believe that deciding the future course of an organization is the task of top management—*a task that cannot and should not be delegated.* Generally, top management will select representatives from the management pool. This may include people from supervisory through executive levels, depending on the size of the organization. Key or senior people in other functional roles (e.g., senior accountant, research scientist) also may be selected to serve on the planning team. At the same time, both input to the process and reactions to decisions that are being reached must be solicited from a broadly representative group of people in the organization.

Who should be involved, what the selection process should be, how to deal with organizational members who feel that they should have been included, how to solicit input and feedback regularly from various segments of the organization, and so on, are matters that need to be addressed with both candor and sensitivity by those initiating the strategic planning process. Among the factors to be considered in making these decisions are the size of the organization, its structure, the various power groups that exist, and the organization's history in dealing with issues of general organizational importance. Again, these issues must be resolved prior to the initiation of any actual planning.

To be effective, a planning team should be able to observe and process its own group dynamics. This means that the planning team should not exceed ten to twelve permanent members. A larger core group simply is not feasible for this type of work.

It is important that *all managers* in your organization, from supervisory through executive, understand the basic phases in strategic planning and also understand that in between each of these phases, many units within the organization (if not all) will be called on to do research, supply data, and/or process data to be used in the planning sequence. The proper role of staff in this effort is to serve as a resource to the management planning group, to conduct research, generate data, and develop alternative ways of integrating and implementing the action steps that emerge from the planning process.

Strategic planning can be vital to the success, and even the future existence, of the organization. Because of the importance of the process and the responsibility assumed by the members of the planning team, it is critical that membership in the planning team be seen as prestigious and important within the organization. If the team does not receive the support and information it needs from the operational parts of the organization, or if the members of the planning team are not allowed to devote the necessary time and energy to the task, the strategic planning process will be thwarted and the entire organization will suffer the consequences.

Time

Another issue that must be dealt with is how long the process will take. As with many such processes, it usually takes longer than anticipated. It often is difficult to ascertain how much consensus already exists within the management team on a variety of issues, how much team building it has undergone, how available the necessary data will be, and what the resources of the organization are for developing data that do not exist. Without the answers to such questions, it is not possible to predict how long the process will take.

Realistically, an organization should expect to spend twelve to twenty full days in the first complete cycle of the planning process, depending on the organization's size and complexity and skills of its planning team—especially its skills in problem identification and problem solving. With each annual repetition of the process, the time may be reduced, but at least twelve days should be set aside.

In an ideal model, the first full process can be completed in nine to twelve months. In such circumstances, the planning group would meet fairly regularly, perhaps every six weeks, for two or three days at a time. Ideally, the group would work effectively toward consensus, develop a mission statement that is rapidly and enthusiastically endorsed by the organization, and then develop strategic plans expeditiously. The resulting action plans then would be developed, tested, integrated, and implemented promptly. But it is more likely that significant stumbling blocks will arise at various points in the sequence, blocks that must be addressed and resolved before the group can move on. For example, in the six weeks between planning-group meetings, various members of the organization may be researching, compiling, and cataloging data that are necessary for the group to consider in the next stage of the process. If such data are readily available, the planning group may decide to meet sooner than a six-week interim. If, however, gathering and processing the required data severely try the resources of the organization, the planning group may decide to postpone its next meeting for a week or two.

Strategic planning has direct impact on budgeting considerations in the organization. In fact, the strategic plan should be the core of the organization's budget for the next year. For that reason, the strategic planning schedule should be established so that the results of the planning process can be fed directly into the budget considerations for the coming year. In the first year of the strategic planning effort, this may require as much as twelve months' lead time; as the process is repeated and becomes refined, nine, six, or even three months may suffice. As the strategic planning process is repeated each year, the gathering and processing of information will become easier, and the relationship between the planning process and budgeting considerations will become more obvious, more automatic, and more harmonious.

Location

Another issue is where the strategic planning sessions should be conducted. The site must be away from the interruptions of daily work. A retreat-type setting often is conducive to the kind of envisioning and confrontation that is involved in strategic planning. The type of facility that might be used for a team-building session probably would be appropriate for a strategic planning session.

Implementation Considerations

Although implementation is the final step of the model, and the functional plans cannot be implemented until integration and checking occur, there is a continual need for implementation throughout the planning process. There are implementation aspects of the planning-to-plan process. If the values audit identifies incongruous values in segments of the organization, these need to be addressed *as soon as they are identified*, not held until the final implementation phase. The mission statement should be distributed for comments and suggestions before it is accepted, and no further planning should be done until there is consensus on the mission statement. Thus, each step of the strategic planning process has implementation considerations and each should be addressed during that stage, not postponed until the final implementation phase.

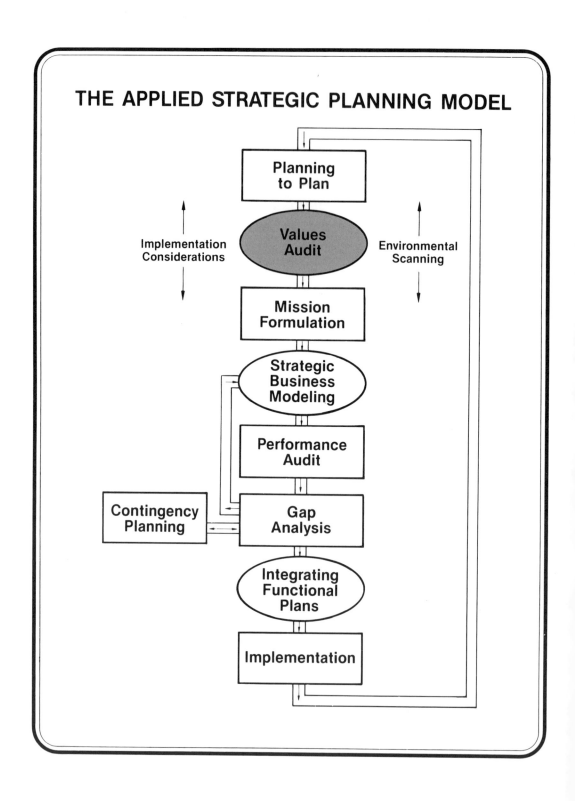

THE APPLIED STRATEGIC PLANNING MODEL

Planning to Plan

Implementation Considerations

Values Audit

Environmental Scanning

Mission Formulation

Strategic Business Modeling

Performance Audit

Contingency Planning

Gap Analysis

Integrating Functional Plans

Implementation

Phase Two:
The Values Audit

A values audit is an examination of the values of the members of the management group within the organization, the current values of the organization, the organization's philosophy of operations, the assumptions that the organization ordinarily uses in its operations, the organization's culture, and, finally, the values of the stakeholders in the organization's future. In this values audit, the planning team moves from an individual focus to a broader examination of the organization and how it works as a social system. The values audit is the *first* formal step of this strategic planning model, an emphasis that is different from that found in most strategic planning models. This stems from our belief that the values of the managers in the organization and the organization as a whole directly impact what can or cannot be implemented in or accomplished by the organization. Values, understanding of mission, and organizational driving forces affect all other stages of the strategic planning process, especially the implementation stage.

Individual Values

This step also involves an examination of the personal values of the individual members of the team. Rokeach (1973) defines a value as "an enduring belief that a specific mode of conduct or end-state of existence is personally or socially preferable to an opposite or converse mode of conduct or end-state of existence" (p. 5). A manager for whom excitement is an important personal value will envision a different organizational future than will a person who holds security as a high personal value. Likewise, the goals and dreams of an individual who holds professional reputation as a value and is less interested in power will be different from those of a person with the opposite priorities.

Organizational values that have become part of the system impact all aspects of the system, regardless of *where* or *who* they come from. For example, the personal style of a manager in one part of the organization may have had enough impact on the people in that unit to have become an assumed value. Likewise, if a majority of the managers are not risk takers, the organizational emphasis may have become one of low-threat, low-risk action, perhaps even without the awareness or sanction of the executive team. In many cases, the values audit will reveal values that have become part of the system in informal, even subtle, ways. This has clear implications for any attempts to implement strategic plans. If a value has become systemic, even though it may not be an official organizational value, it can affect the implementation of any part of the plan. The job of the planning team at this stage, then, is to identify what is happening in the system, acknowledge what exists, and remember that information later when the team begins to consider implementation issues.

These differences have clear implications for the organization's future, design, decision-making processes, and even for work in the organization. If the differences are not identified, clarified, and resolved early in the planning process, there may be little or no agreement about how the organization's future meets the personal expectations of the individual members of the management group. Once there is clarity and consensus on individual values, the strategic planning process can move ahead. Indeed, strategic planning is, in some respects, a value-clarification exercise, and the actual strategic plan for an organization represents the operational implementation of the consensual values of the management team.

Organizational Values

Once the individual values of the management team have been worked through, the values of the organization must be dealt with. These are evidenced by the end state or mode of behavior that the organization appears to prefer; but because organizational values are not easily tapped or identified, it may require some exploration by the planning team to determine, for example, how much risk taking the organization should engage in or whether "equity" is a strongly held organizational value. All organizations have values and these values must be identified as part of the strategic planning process. Any strategic plan that attempts to ignore or is inconsistent with or contrary to the existing *organizational* values is extremely unlikely to succeed and may well backfire.

Both the development of such questions and the process of searching for answers require some facilitative expertise. Almost all organizations need to enlist the services of a consultant who is skilled in facilitating group processes. This person may be a member of the organization's training or human resource development staff or may be an external consultant.

Philosophy of Operations

An organization's values are organized and codified into its philosophy of operations, that is, the way the organization approaches its work. Some organizations have explicit, formal statements of philosophy, such as the Five Principles of Mars, the multinational candy corporation (see Figure 1). These formal statements integrate the organization's values with the way it does business. Value-driven organizations such as Mars spend a good deal of time and energy disseminating and tracking the impact of their philosophy on all organizational behavior. All employees are expected to know the philosophy and to use it in their daily work, and there are serious sanctions against any violation of the philosophy by an organizational member.

1. **Quality**
   The consumer is our boss, quality is our work, and value for money is our goal.
2. **Responsibility**
   As individuals, we demand total responsibility from ourselves; as associates, we support the responsibilities of others.
3. **Mutuality**
   A mutual benefit is a shared benefit; a shared benefit will endure.
4. **Efficiency**
   We use resources to the fullest, waste nothing, and do only what we can do best.
5. **Freedom**
   We need freedom to shape our future; we need profit to remain free.

Figure 1. The Five Principles of Mars

All organizations have philosophies of operation, whether or not these are stated explicitly, and all organizations disseminate their philosophies and judge members on conformance to philosophy. If your organization's philosophy of operations is implicit, it is necessary to make it explicit as part of the strategic planning process. The strategic plan must fit the philosophy or the philosophy must be modified—a difficult task at best.

An organization's philosophy of operations includes a series of assumptions about the way things work and the way in which decisions are made. Such assumptions in the profit-making sector include "No profit can be made doing business with the government" or "Allowing a labor union to organize our hourly production people would destroy this company." In the nonprofit sector, typical assumptions are: "If we do not spend all of this year's budget, they will cut us next time" and "You have to go along to get along." Some general assumptions that you may have heard are that the organization's growth is assured by an expanding and more affluent population or that there never will be a satisfactory substitute for the organization's major product or service.

Unless such assumptions are examined in terms of their current validity and relevance—whether or not they ever were true or relevant—the organization will continue to assume that they are true and operate accordingly. Thus, an important part of the strategic planning process is to identify the assumptions that the organization makes about its environment, its operations, and how things do or should work and to examine their validity.

One function of the strategic planning consultant is to keep a record of organizational assumptions as they are observed and, at the appropriate time in the planning process, to present them to the group for examination. There must be commitment from the senior executives of the organization to this process, so that the consultant has the credibility and the "go ahead" to question, examine, and confront the issues under consideration.

Organizational Culture

The management team members' values, the organization's values, its philosophy of operations, and its operating assumptions all produce the organization's culture, which Marvin Bowers, former managing director of McKinsey and Company, defines as "the way we do things around here" (Deal & Kennedy, 1982, p. 4). Your organization's culture provides the social surroundings in and through which the organization performs its work. It actually guides you and all the organization's members in decision making, task behavior, and practically everything else you do in the organization.

There is no single index of an organization's culture, but the anthropological evidence is everywhere. An outsider first experiences your organization's culture in its physical structure and then in how those guarding the organization's boundaries—guards, parking-lot attendants, receptionists, and the like—behave toward them. The war stories told about the heroics of the organization in the "good (or bad) old days," the organizational heroes and villains, the rites and rituals of the organization, and the symbols that the organization uses to portray itself to the public all provide information about its culture. This information should be analyzed and integrated into the strategic planning process.

If the strategic plan is not integrated with the culture of the organization, it is doomed to failure. The strategic planning team also should examine its *own* culture and realize how it affects the process of planning the organization's future.

Stakeholder Analysis

Finally, an audit of organizational values requires a stakeholder analysis. Stakeholders are those individuals, groups, and organizations who will be impacted by or interested in your organization's strategic plan. They must be identified, and their concerns must be determined (that is, how their resources, status, freedom of action, relationships, and activities may appear to them to be impacted by shifts or changes in the organization's direction). Stakeholders typically include: employees (including managers), clients or customers, suppliers, governments, unions, creditors, owners, shareholders, and members of the community who *believe* that they have a stake in your organization, regardless of whether or not such a belief is accurate or reasonable.

Once the stakeholders are identified, the impact of various future states on different stakeholders can be considered. It is important that the planning team identify the significant stakeholders early in the values audit. If this is not done until later in the process, a more selective list may emerge. The stakeholders are the various constituencies that need to be considered by the strategic planning team.

The values audit is the most important and the most difficult part of the planning process. It requires an in-depth analysis of the most fundamental beliefs that underlie organizational life and organizational decision making. Such confrontation can be a long and painful experience. But without such work, differences in values, philosophy, and assumptions will surface continually in the planning process and block forward movement. Once these issues are successfully clarified and resolved, the differences do not interfere with the planning process and it is relatively easy to move to the next phase of the process.

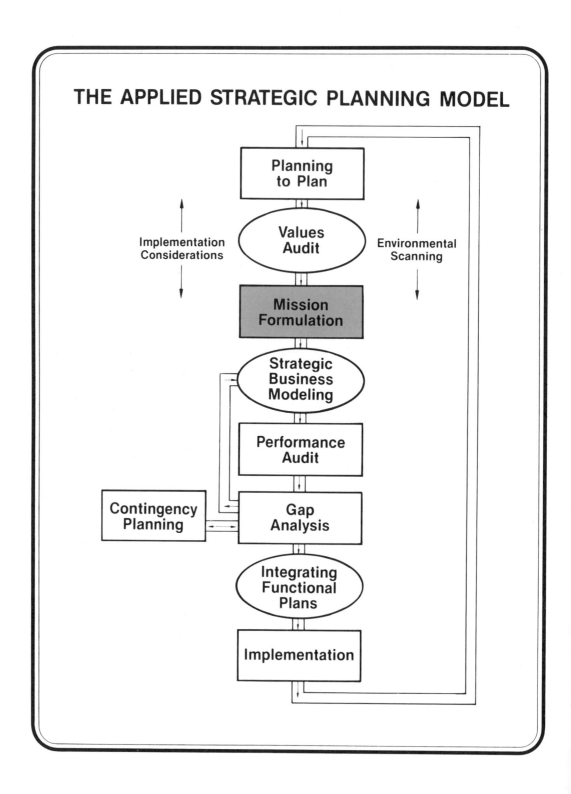

THE APPLIED STRATEGIC PLANNING MODEL

Planning to Plan

Implementation Considerations

Values Audit

Environmental Scanning

Mission Formulation

Strategic Business Modeling

Performance Audit

Contingency Planning

Gap Analysis

Integrating Functional Plans

Implementation

Phase Three:
Mission Formulation

When there is informed consensus about the underlying values and beliefs that will drive the organization, the planning team can turn its attention to the next phase of the process: mission formulation. This involves developing a clear statement of what business the organization is in, a concise declaration of the purpose or function that the organization is attempting to fulfill in society or the economy.

In formulating its mission, an organization must answer three primary questions: (a) *What* function does the organization perform?; (b) For *whom* does the organization perform this function?; and (c) *How* does the organization go about filling this function?

"What?"

Most organizations tend to answer the "what" question in terms of the goods or services produced. Manufacturers of detergents see themselves as in the "soap business," and gasoline producers see themselves as in the "oil business." As Levitt (1975) pointed out a decade ago, such myopia prevents organizations both from seeing new opportunities for growth and expansion and from responding to threats and challenges. The recommended alternative is to answer the question in terms of the customer or client needs that the organization attempts to meet. If your organization identifies itself as meeting certain public needs, it will be more sensitive to identifying and treating those needs, more likely to develop new products and services to meet those needs, and less likely to experience obsolescence and decline. If a detergent manufacturer sees itself as being in the business of providing a mechanism for helping people to clean their garments, or if gasoline producers see themselves as being in the business of providing sources of energy to consumers, many new options are open to them—ultrasonic cleaners, solar and wind power generators, and so on. Successful organizations try to identify value-satisfying goods and services that meet the needs of the public and include these considerations in their mission formulations. The major issue in mission formulation typically is achieving consensus on how broadly or narrowly to answer the "what" question.

"Who?"

Identifying the "who" is the second concern of mission formulation. No organization, no matter how large, can meet all the needs of all possible clients or customers. The mission formulation requires a clear identification of what portion of the total potential customer base your organization identifies as its primary target. The process of sorting out the potential customer or client base and identifying which portion should be sought out by the organization typically is called market segmentation.

Markets can be segmented in many ways: geographically, financially, ethnically, and so on. The needs of Sun Belt consumers are different from those of Frost Belt consumers. Federal Express serves customers who are willing to spend more than the price of ordinary postage to ensure next-day delivery of packages. Kosher foods have devout consumers, as do soul foods. General Motors has five traditional automobile lines, each designed for consumers in different economic strata.

"How?"

Once the planning team has identified what your organization does and for whom, the next step is to decide *how* the organization will proceed to achieve this mission. The "how" can involve a marketing strategy, such as being the low-cost producer or the technological leader or the high-quality manufacturer; it may involve a distribution system, such as regional warehouses or evening classes in factories or no-appointment medical treatment facilities. It may involve customer service or personalized selling or any of a variety of processes through which an organization can deliver products or services to a defined consumer group.

Driving Forces

One more important factor must be considered as part of mission formulation: the identification and prioritizing of the organization's *driving forces*. Tregoe and Zimmerman (1980) identify nine basic categories of driving forces. These are:

1. *Products or Services Offered.* The organization is committed primarily to a product or service such as retail banking, corn-sugar refining, or automotive manufacturing, and limits its strategy to more of that product or service, done better.
2. *Market Needs.* Market-driven organizations continually survey potential customers to discover unfilled needs for goods and services. Once these are identified, the organization develops products to fill those needs.
3. *Technology.* Organizations that are technology driven continually try to develop products and services based on the latest scientific breakthroughs.

4. *Production Capability.* Capacity-driven organizations have a primary commitment to keeping their existing production capability utilized, e.g., to have hospital beds filled or to have aluminum ingots on the back loading dock ready to be shipped.

5. *Method of Sale.* The method of sale, such as door-to-door selling, direct mail, premiums and bonus programs, and so on, directs the strategy of these organizations.

6. *Method of Distribution.* Some organizations are driven by their current method of distribution, which may be regional warehouses, manufacturer's representatives, pipelines, and so on.

7. *Natural Resources.* Certain types of organizations are driven by their dependency on natural resources such as coal, timber, petroleum, metals, or land.

8. *Size and Growth.* Organizations that are driven by set goals regarding size and growth constantly strive for continuing significant growth above current performance.

9. *Profit/Return on Investment.* Some organizations set high requirements about profit margins or return on investments and make decisions to achieve those goals.

Although all nine of these areas should be considered in strategic planning, Tregoe and Zimmerman believe that an organization must be clear about which factor is its driving force. They believe that when decisions are to be made that require choosing among these nine considerations, the decision makers in the organization must have mutual understanding about whether their goal is to emphasize profit, or research and development, or the development of a sales force in order to achieve growth, or some other factor that will be the single driving force behind the organization's strategy.

We, on the other hand, have found it to be more useful to have the strategic planning team prioritize the driving forces from one to nine in terms of their perceived relative importance, rather than to attempt to identify a single one. The importance of gaining consensus on these priorities should be apparent. Most major, strategic decisions that organizations make involve the allocation of resources according to a set of priorities. When there are inadequate resources or the choices are incompatible, the rank order of the nine strategic areas will determine how resources are to be allocated or which direction will be chosen. A consensual rank order, with the most important driving force in first place, enables the planning team to make otherwise difficult decisions rather easily.

Mission Statement

Once the questions of "what," "who," and "how" are answered and the driving force identified, these elements can be woven into the organization's mission statement. This should be a brief (one hundred words or less) statement that identifies the basic business the organization is in. The mission statement, which should be known to all members of your organization and understood by them, answers the questions of what the organization does, for whom, and how, and identifies the organization's major, strategic, driving force. By providing this information for both internal and external use, the organization identifies its distinctive competence(s)—those distinctive products or services offered by the organization that set it apart from its competitors. The following is an example of a reasonably effective mission statement:

> The Alpha Corporation is a low-cost manufacturer and marketer of consumable food-service items for home and industrial use. We intend to maintain our position as a market leader by meeting customer needs and providing a high level of quality and service while maintaining a sufficiently high level of earnings to satisfy our investors.

Developing a mission statement is an extremely difficult and time-consuming task, but one that the planning group must complete before moving to the next step. Developing, editing, and reaching consensus on such a statement requires skill, patience, and understanding. However, the mission statement provides an enormously valuable management tool to the organization: it clearly charts its future direction and establishes a basis for organizational decision making.

Unit Mission Statements

The next step is for each *major unit* of your organization to develop its own mission statement. Unit mission statements should be more focused and more limited than that of the total organization, but they clearly must be derived from the organizational statement.

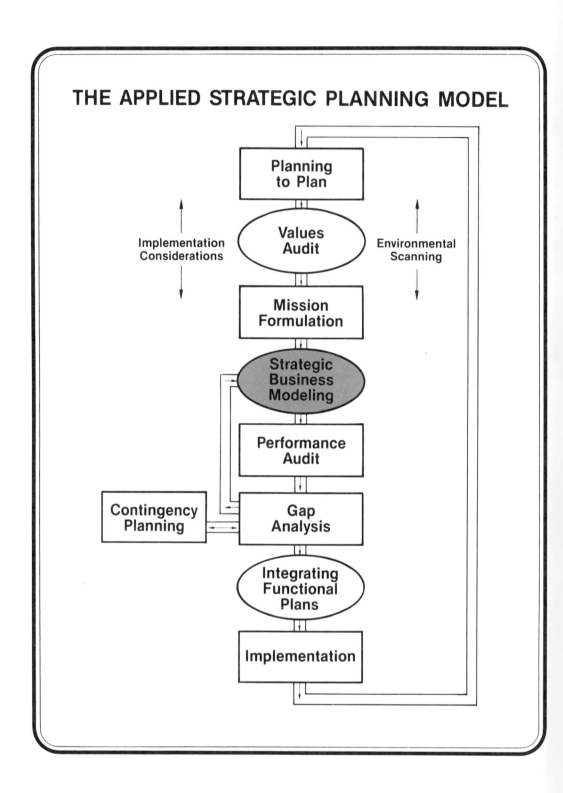

THE APPLIED STRATEGIC PLANNING MODEL

Planning to Plan

Values Audit

Implementation Considerations

Environmental Scanning

Mission Formulation

Strategic Business Modeling

Performance Audit

Contingency Planning

Gap Analysis

Integrating Functional Plans

Implementation

22

Phase Four:
Strategic Business Modeling

Strategic business modeling is the process by which the organization more specifically defines success in the context of the business(es) it wants to be in, how that success will be measured, and what will be done to achieve it, consistent with the newly established mission statement. The strategic business model includes the following:

1. The strategic *profile.* The components of this profile include orientation toward risk, the approach to competition, and an expression of the critical success indicators. Examples of these critical success indicators might be: increase after-tax profits to 5 percent, reduce annual turnover to less than 9 percent, and pay no more than 20 percent of net income in taxes. The strategic profile should identify the business(es) the organization wants to be in *three to five years in the future,* including the critical success indicators such as profitability, market penetration, liquidity, and so on.

2. Statements of *how* the proposed objectives will be achieved, in specific segments. For example, the objective "reduce the effective tax rate to 25 percent" will be achieved by (a) sheltering 70 percent of income, (b) purchasing $500,000 worth of capital equipment, and so on. This may include a model of the future organization, a statement about how much organizational risk taking will be involved, how competitors will be approached, and how other critical areas of organizational activity will be managed. The specific products and services that the organization proposes to provide and the specific markets to which they will be aimed also should be identified.

As an example, the Alpha Corporation's strategic profile may include: "increase sales 15 percent a year for five years." With this target established, the second part of strategic business modeling is to define how it will be done. At this point the issues of plant capacity, marketing strategies, product development or acquisitions, capital, and human resource needs can be considered. These would then be detailed in a later phase called "integrating functional plans." The "how" consideration would include the identification of the various routes by which each organizational objective could be met, a cost/benefit analysis of each, and selection of the particular strategies that are most likely to achieve the organization's objectives. The cost-benefit analysis is an important consideration here. For example, in organizations that sell products or services, growth often is defined as "increasing the market share." Because growth requires initial expenditures (e.g., for product development, storage, advertising, expansion of sales staff, etc.), profit is not generated immediately. The strategic planning team must determine what the organization will need to spend (and is willing to spend) to achieve each point of increased market share, and the strategic profile ultimately will include that level of growth that the organization can afford to strive for in the coming year.

It is important that the strategic planning team envision the organization's future *prior* to conducting an in-depth analysis of its current performance. The resulting target should reflect the values and major directions developed in the earlier stages of the planning process.

That applied strategic planning is distinctively different from long-range planning becomes most clear in the strategic business modeling process. Long-range planning tends to be merely an extension of what an organization is doing already. The Alpha Corporation may plan to sell more units through its existing distribution network. A hospital may plan to open a suburban branch. Both of these plans involve only slight variations in or expansions of the product or service offered in existing markets. Such typical long-range planning often is myopic and unduly constraining. When an organization focuses heavily on that area of the market that it currently occupies, it overlooks other possible markets.

Considerations

Several considerations are, however, critical to the success of this stage. First, the modeling must be congruent with and build on the identified values and mission of the organization. Second, the modeling must be done in a context of proactive futuring: the belief that, although no one can fully predict the future, it is possible to anticipate significant aspects of the future, to conceptualize a desired end state for the organization taking those aspects of the future into account, and to work proactively to make that desired future state occur. Within this context, the organization takes responsibility for its own future rather than assigning that responsibility to unseen external forces.

The third consideration is that although strategic business modeling involves a heavy emphasis on focused creativity—a free-flowing generation of ideas that involves many alternative options for the organization to consider, success in this phase of the process is most likely to be attained when there is maximum creative output within *realistic* boundaries. There is little or no point in the Alpha Corporation's planning team considering a new business focus unless the corporation has expertise and resources in that business. In their book, *In Search of Excellence: Lessons from America's Best-Run Companies*, Peters and Waterman (1982) call this "stick to the knitting." A model commonly used in this regard utilizes the previously made identification of the "What," "Who," and "How" aspects of the organization's mission and places these elements in a triangular arrangement (see Figure 2). The implication of this model is that an organization should not attempt to change more than *one* of these three elements in considering a new business focus.

Figure 2. Three Basic Elements of the Organizational Mission

For example, a manufacturer of skiis and skiing equipment might develop a new product (ski goggles) for its existing customers (skiing enthusiasts) and utilize its existing sales staff and method of distribution (sporting-goods stores) to reach those customers or clients. Or the organization may choose to expand its sales of skiis by advertising them in a direct-mail catalog. In either case, only one basic aspect of the organization's functioning would be altered to accommodate the new venture.

Another model illustrates a related, and generally accepted, tenet in organizational planning (see Figure 3).

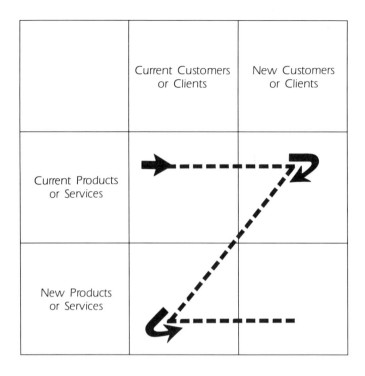

	Current Customers or Clients	New Customers or Clients
Current Products or Services		
New Products or Services		

Figure 3. The "Z" Model[1]

The arrows in the figure illustrate an increasing degree of risk as they follow the Z-shaped path. That is, starting with existing products and customers, there is increased risk in attempting to cultivate new customers; there is even greater risk in attempting to develop new products; and there is the greatest degree of risk in attempting to develop new products for a new customer base.

A primary purpose of the strategic business model is that it provides the organization with a standard by which to gauge a number of business decisions. If goals are stated formally and quantitatively, the degree of success in reaching those goals can be measured more easily.

---

[1]The "Z" model of increased risk was developed by John M. Simonds of Martin-Simonds Associates, Seattle, Washington. The matrix of "current clients-current services" originally appeared in H. Igor Ansoff, "Strategies for Diversification," *Harvard Business Review*, September-October, 1957, pp. 113-124.

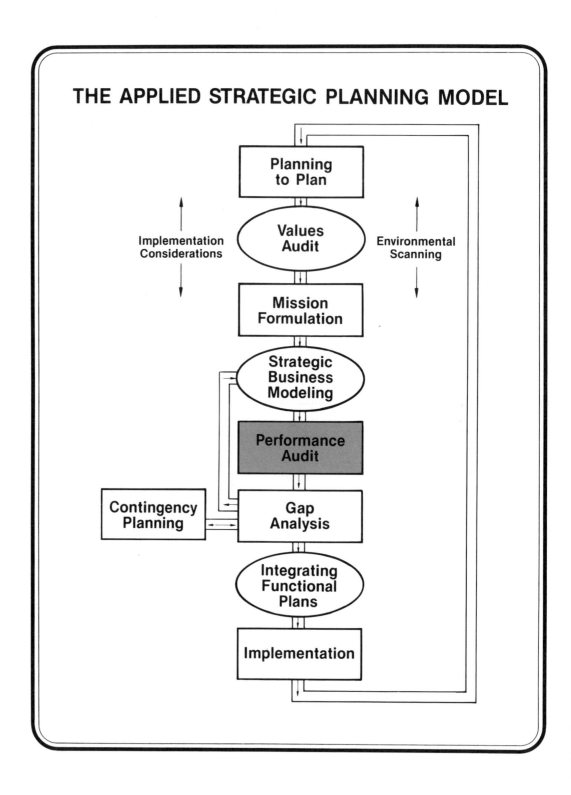

THE APPLIED STRATEGIC PLANNING MODEL

Planning to Plan

Implementation Considerations

Values Audit

Environmental Scanning

Mission Formulation

Strategic Business Modeling

Performance Audit

Contingency Planning

Gap Analysis

Integrating Functional Plans

Implementation

Phase Five:
Performance Audit

The performance audit examines the *recent* performance of your organization in terms of the basic performance indices (such as growth, production, quality, service, profit, return on investment, cash flow, and so on) that have been identified in the strategic profile. These are the key indices that tell the planning team what is happening in and to the organization and its field of endeavor. The "focused creativity" encouraged in strategic business modeling frequently results in some exciting goals. The purpose of the performance audit is to establish the benchmark of capability against which these goals can be tested.

Any data that can help the organization to better understand its present capabilities for doing its work should be included in the performance analysis. Such data might include life cycles of existing products, employee productivity, scrap rate, inventory turnover, facilities (including capacity and condition), and management capability. The important question that the performance audit must answer is whether or not the organization has the capability to successfully implement its strategic business plan and achieve its mission. Therefore, in planning the performance audit, special attention must be paid to obtaining the hard data that will indicate the organization's capacity to move in the identified strategic directions.

Competitor Analysis

The performance audit should include information about the forces outside the organization that might impact the strategic business model. One of the most important sets of data is the competitor analysis, which profiles organizations that are in the same business or aiming for the same market segment of clients or consumers. The competitor analysis should include "creative crossovers"—items that are sold or services that are delivered for similar reasons. For example, one of the chief competitors of Cross pens during the holiday season is not another pen manufacturer but the billfold industry, because both pen-and-pencil sets and billfolds are frequently purchased as holiday gifts for men. Thus, the performance audit will include data derived from the organization's own experience as well as data about the experience of the overall industry or field of service of which the organization is a part. These data later will be compared directly with the indices of success or growth identified in the strategic business model.

One way to understand a competitor is offered by Porter (1980) and is illustrated in Figure 4.

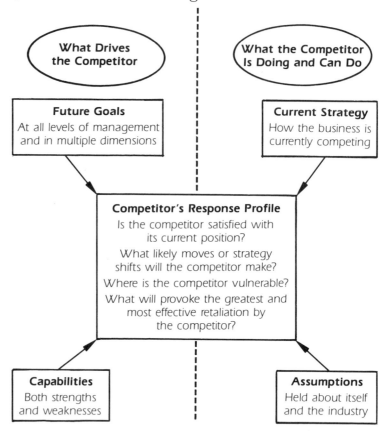

Figure 4. The Components of a Competitor Analysis[2]

This competitor analysis focuses on the competitor's current position and strategy (the right side of Figure 4)—information that usually is available, at least informally. In doing a competitor analysis, however, your organization also must strive to understand the underlying goals and assumptions that drive each competitor (indicated on the left side of the figure). Such understanding enables your organization to anticipate the competitor's future strategy, including its response to *your* competitive efforts. As Porter points out, such an analysis will not only help you to understand your competition but also will help you to understand what conclusions your competitors are likely to draw about your organization.

---

[2]From M.E. Porter, *Competitive Strategy: Techniques for Analyzing Industries and Competitors.* New York: The Free Press, 1980, p. 49. Used with permission.

Data collected as part of the competitor analysis (and from an ongoing organizational process of environmental scanning) may include who is going into or out of the business that your organization is engaged in, the profitability of competitor companies, the market share held by each of the other companies, their customer or client loyalty, the images of various competitors in the marketplace, and so on.

There are many sources of information about actual and potential competitors. These include published materials such as competitor's annual reports, trade or industry publications, governmental reports, patent records, speeches made by the executives or managers of competitor companies, etc. Numerous electronic data bases, such as Economic Information Systems, will provide information about other companies' dollar volume of output, number of employees, share of the market, industrial facilities, and so on. These services charge a fee, but are legal sources of information. More informal sources of data include people and exhibits at trade shows, help-wanted ads, technical meetings, and customer surveys or inquiries. The distributors and suppliers used by the competition often are excellent sources of data, as are their advertising agencies. "Shopping" the competition is another tried-and-true means of obtaining data and may include reverse engineering, in which one breaks down the competitor's product and analyzes it in order to learn more about it. As an example, the United States military forces have purchased captured Russian military equipment from other countries in order to conduct reverse engineering studies and field trials with the Russian equipment. Obviously, many companies are unlikely to cooperate in sharing information that could aid their competitors, and many actively attempt to prevent their competitors from learning about their present and planned strategies and products. However, there are ways to obtain some pertinent information without resorting to unethical or illegal practices.

Because the competitor analysis usually will require some research, and—as an additional benefit—to increase awareness of the marketplace, we recommend that each member of the planning team have responsibility for conducting an analysis of one to three competitors. This will become an ongoing responsibility of all managers and key personnel in the organization. It may be useful to formulate a work sheet that all managers can use in researching their portions of the competition. A manager may choose to delegate portions of this effort, as appropriate, but every manager in the organization should be prepared to incorporate portions of the competitor analysis—as well as the generation of information for other components of the performance audit—into his or her work flow every year.

SBU Analysis

One major emphasis of the performance-audit analysis should be a strategic business unit (SBU) analysis. A strategic business unit is a division, department, or product line—a budgeting or profit center—that is a business unto itself within the organization; for example, the loan department in a bank, the home-furnishings division of a large department store, or the pharmacy in a large "drugstore." The SBU analysis should identify which aspects of the business are losing money, how strengths can be reinforced and weaknesses eliminated, and so on. In addition, the managers or key personnel of two or more strategic business units may monitor the same competitor in regard to their *areas* of the business.

Other Data

In addition, market research, examination of macro and micro economic trends, and studies of work-force availability should be included in the data gathered for the performance audit. This information should include a consideration of both current and future trends—a longitudinal perspective. In the game of chess, this is called "thinking down board," i.e., "If I do this, my competitor will do that, then I will need to. . . ."

Much, but not all, of the data required for the performance audit will be available in organizations that have good management information systems, including financial reporting systems. Furthermore, although data bases may be available (inside or outside the organization), the organization may need to hire or reassign financial staff to research, validate, combine, analyze, and report the data. This is a crunch point in many organizations: the ability—in terms of time, personnel, expertise, and so on—to handle and report on the data. However, it should be obvious to everyone in the organization who is directly or indirectly involved in the strategic planning process that the data are a critical part of the process and that something must be *done* with the data that are to be utilized. As the strategic planning process becomes part of the ongoing organizational functioning, appropriate financial units within the organization may absorb most, if not all, of this task. Initially, or in smaller organizations, the task may be dispersed in-house or the data may be sent out to be organized and reported by a firm that specializes in such functions.

The role of the strategic planning consultant in this process is to help the planning team to do problem solving regarding how the data will be collected and by whom, how tasks will be dispersed, and how the data will be handled once it has been collected.

It should be obvious by now that the performance audit and subsequent analysis are some of the most detailed and time-consuming aspects of the strategic planning process. However, without this important, detailed information, the basis for planning is incomplete and shaky. In addition, the need for candor, openness, and nondefensiveness during the performance audit should not be underestimated. An organization that fools itself during the performance audit is almost certain to find itself with an unworkable plan. Obviously, under such circumstances, the time and effort put into the strategic planning process will result in a travesty.

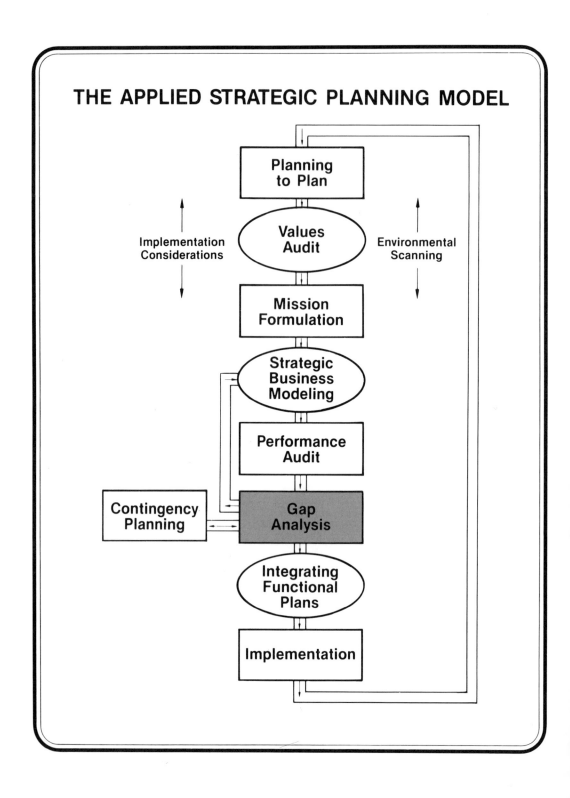

THE APPLIED STRATEGIC PLANNING MODEL

Planning to Plan

Values Audit

Implementation Considerations

Environmental Scanning

Mission Formulation

Strategic Business Modeling

Performance Audit

Contingency Planning

Gap Analysis

Integrating Functional Plans

Implementation

Phase Six:
Gap Analysis

As was mentioned previously, the gap analysis is a comparison of the data generated during the performance audit with the strategic profile. If there is a substantial discrepancy between the profile and the organization's capacity to achieve that profile, the planning team must *return* to the strategic business modeling phase and rework the model until the gap between the profile and the organization's capacity to achieve it is reduced to a more realistic size. In other words, the gap analysis is a "reality test" of the strategic business model indices. If the strategic business model stipulates 28 percent growth and the performance audit reveals an average growth rate for the organization of 3.5 percent over several years, or if the strategic business model calls for an increase in profit of 12 percent and the performance audit reveals that the average annual profit increase for the entire industry is only 4 percent, then the planning team will know that it is time to re-evaluate the strategic business model in light of the new data. Thus, the key indices of success are first identified during the *strategic business modeling,* and their feasibility is checked later—with the information generated during the *performance audit*—by means of the *gap analysis.*

Comparison and Modification

For this reason, the Applied Strategic Planning Model depicts an arrow running backward from the gap analysis to the strategic business modeling phase, in addition to the arrows running forward from strategic business modeling to the performance audit and then to the gap analysis. Each and every "gap" requires a re-evaluation of the applicable portion of the strategic business model, so several repetitions of this process may be necessary before the gaps can be closed. Occasionally, the mission statement may even need to be modified in the process.

If the gap analysis reveals a substantial disparity between the performance audit and the strategic profile or the strategies identified for achieving it, the design or functioning of the organization may need to be re-examined. Obviously, either the strategic business model or the organization or both need to be modified in order to close the gaps between the plan and the organization's capacity.

A significant part of the gap analysis is the comparison of the strategic business model with the outcome of the values audit and the mission statement, in order to ascertain that the things the organization is proposing to do are consistent with its culture. As has been noted earlier, plans that do not take into account and build on the organization's culture are not likely to succeed. This portion of the gap analysis requires the same degree of openness, candor, and confrontation that should have typified the original values audit. The gap analysis is important because it tests the organization's "wants" against reality; in effect, it is the anchor that keeps the plan from floating off in an unguided, or misguided, direction.

THE APPLIED STRATEGIC PLANNING MODEL

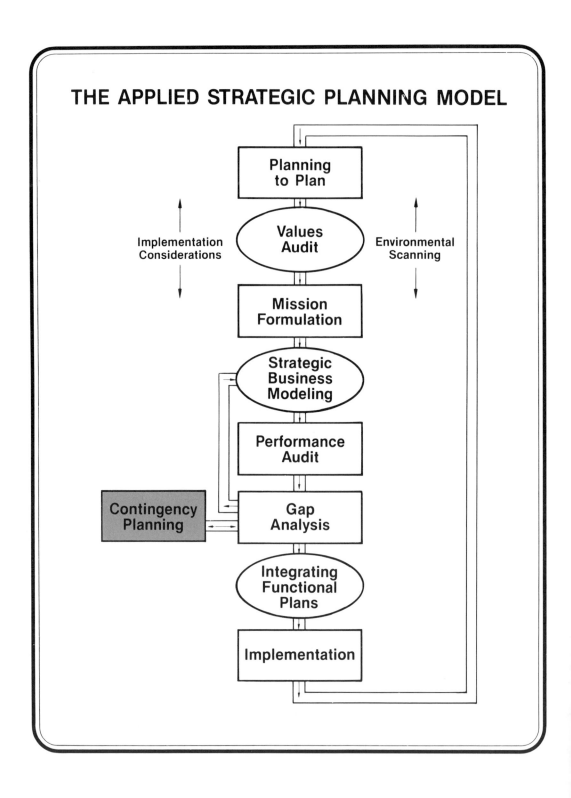

Phase Seven:
Contingency Planning

As part of the gap analysis, your strategic planning team will identify the major opportunities of and threats to your organization as well as the key indicators that suggest that these opportunities or threats are likely to become realities. Although these events or conditions are not highly likely to occur, they are considered because they will necessitate changes if they do occur. Contingency planning is placed *below* the other, linear, phases of the model because those phases are based on high-probability assumptions.

Aside from "universal" concerns such as war, economic collapse, and the like, each type of business or organization is subject to a specific set of contingencies that must be planned for. For example, producers of building materials are heavily influenced by new housing starts which, in turn, are a function of interest rates and general economic conditions. In developing its strategic business model, a producer of building materials may identify several alternative futures, each based on different volumes of housing starts. Housing starts, in turn, are influenced by a variety of governmental actions; the elimination of mortgage deductions on personal income taxes clearly would be a threat to housing starts, while a large governmental program to subsidize single-family homes would be an opportunity. The strategic business model of the building-materials producer would assume that neither of these two events would be likely to occur, but contingency plans would be developed on the basis of both possibilities. Other contingencies that could affect an organization include changes in tax laws, dramatic changes in the marketplace, and the loss of certain key managers or executives.

Contingency planning is based on the assumption that the ability to forecast accurately the significant factors that will affect the organization is somewhat limited, especially in terms of variations in those factors. However, the planning team should be able to identify the factors themselves, such as interest rates, employment, housing starts, foreign currency exchange rates, and so on, and develop alternative plans based on possible variations in these factors. The word "alternative" is important; the planning team should develop several options for each contingency, and these options should involve different types of solutions. For example, if an identified contingency is "the possible incapacitation of the president of the organization," contingency plans could include succession planning and training, a "key-man" insurance policy, and arranging for an outside management expert to fill the gap during the crisis. Thus, the purpose of contingency planning is to provide the organization with a variety of options, a variety of business-modeling strategies that can be used with a variety of scenarios, each of which can be evaluated and planned for.

Key Indicators and "Trigger Points"

The contingency-planning process also should identify a number of key indicators that will trigger an awareness of the need to re-examine the adequacy of the strategy currently being followed. A "trigger point" could be an event such as the warehouse burning down, a major supplier's failure to renew a contract, a competitor's introduction of a new product, a turnover of key personnel, or a change in the organization's salaries-to-revenue ratio. Trigger points also can be positive occurrences, such as a large, unexpected demand for a newly introduced product or service or a sharp, positive turnaround in the economy that offers the possibility for expansion and growth.

When a trigger point is identified as having been reached, two levels of response should be generated:

1. Higher-level monitoring. No precipitant action should be taken; in fact, no action may be required. However, the *possibility* of a need for a change in main-line assumptions should be noted, and indicators should be watched.
2. Action. At this level, the decision is made that conditions are different, and some contingency plan is implemented or some aspect of a strategy is modified.

Contingency planning is based on the realization that the old joke about "Plan B" is not really a joke. As Louis Pasteur once observed, "Chance favors the prepared mind."

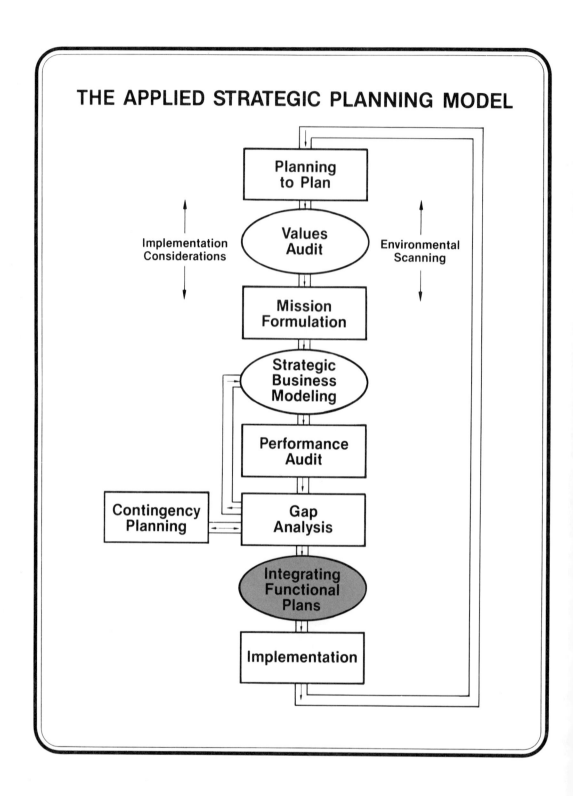

THE APPLIED STRATEGIC PLANNING MODEL

Planning to Plan

Implementation Considerations

Values Audit

Environmental Scanning

Mission Formulation

Strategic Business Modeling

Performance Audit

Contingency Planning

Gap Analysis

Integrating Functional Plans

Implementation

Phase Eight:
Integrating Functional Plans

Once the gap analysis has been completed and the planning team agrees that the gap between the strategic business model and the organization's capacity is a manageable one, planning should be delegated to functional units of the organization, each of which should be called on to develop detailed, functional plans, with a budget and a clear-cut timetable for execution. In the typical organization, there would be a financial plan, a product plan, a marketing plan, a human resources plan, a capital-equipment plan, and so on. This should be accomplished *before* the overall budget decisions for the organization are made, so that the final plans can be integrated into the budget considerations. Each line manager generally will serve as the liaison between the strategic planning team and his or her own functional unit.

For example, in a human resources plan, current and future needs for staffing on the managerial, supervisory, technical, production, and administrative levels would be developed for the time period of the plan. Such a plan would take into account employee turnover, staffing needs, recruitment and training programs, and costs, and would include contingency plans. Each functional unit should be provided with copies of the organization's mission statement and any other information derived from previous stages of the planning process that is necessary for it to complete its functional plan.

Each unit's functional plan then must be checked against the organizational values audit and mission statement to determine whether the proposed actions and directions are consistent with what the organization has said it wants to be. This check may reveal a need for further clarification of the values, mission, and strategic business model of the organization so that all plans are developed with the same overall objectives and assumptions.

Agreement To Share Resources

Each plan developed by a functional group in the organization also must be understood and agreed to by each of the other functional groups in the organization. Again, this usually is done by the managers through established reporting lines. It is done as part of the annual budget meeting, through the organizational budgeting process. This process often is difficult, because once the model is developed and plans are made, each part of the organization begins to compete for limited resources in order to attain its objectives, achieve the planned growth, and so on. Several departments simultaneously may require the services of the graphics department, need a new computer program, or produce something that requires the support of the sales staff or the mailing department. All these actions have timing and budget implications as well. It is imperative that the managers of all the functional units within the organization understand the impact of such competition and agree to the planned allocation of resources both to their units and to the other functional units.

Putting It All Together

The planning team then will identify the gaps in and between the combined plans, how these can be closed, and what the impact of the gaps might be on the successful execution of the strategic business model. The integration of the functional plans involves putting together all the pieces in order to ascertain how the overall plan will work and where the potential trouble spots are. This integration is a major portion of the budgetary process.

THE APPLIED STRATEGIC PLANNING MODEL

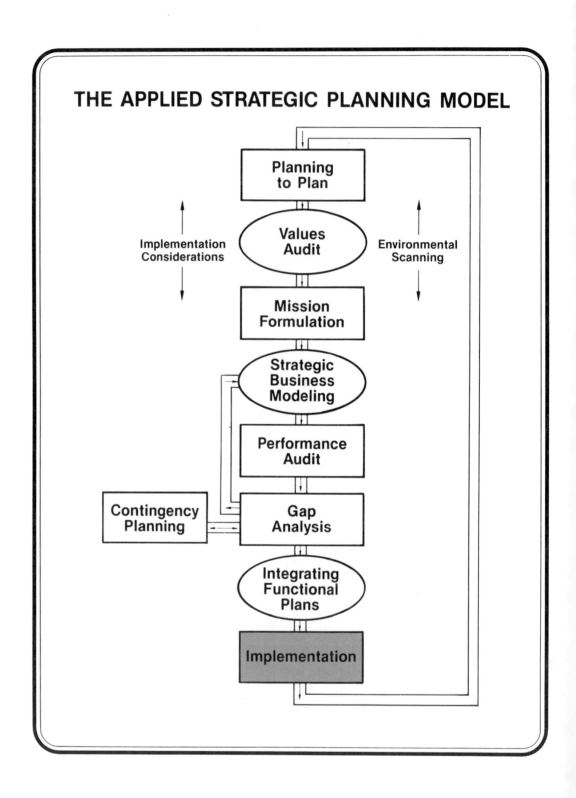

Phase Nine:
Implementation

The final implementation of the strategic plan involves the initiation of the several action plans designed at the functional level and their integration at the top of the organization. This may, for example, involve new construction, initiation of management development or technical training, increased research and development, marketing of new products or services, and so on. In effect, implementation is the strategic plan handed from the planning team to the functional managers. All parts of the organization should feel that there is activity on all levels of the organization that will bring about the successful completion of the organization's mission.

The most important test of implementation, however, is the degree to which organizational members, especially managers, integrate the strategic plan into their everyday management decisions. A strategic plan is being implemented when the initial response of a manager confronted by a decision is to consider whether an answer is found in the organization's strategic plan. Although guidelines for every decision will not be provided by the planning process, consideration of the plan as a first step is the best evidence of the plan's implementation.

This final step is by no means the only point of implementation. As the Applied Strategic Planning Model indicates, implementation considerations should be addressed throughout the planning process, because in some cases implementation will be required immediately.

THE APPLIED STRATEGIC PLANNING MODEL

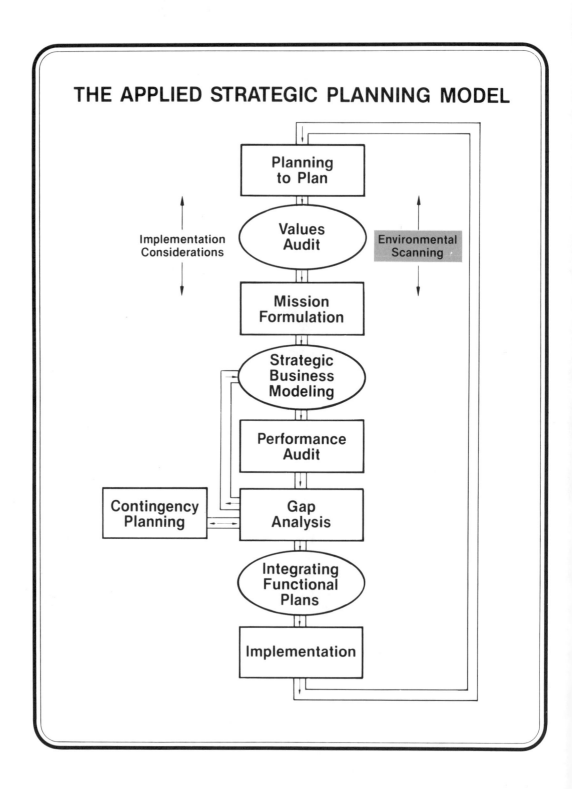

Environmental Scanning

Throughout their existence, organizations need to be aware of what is happening in their environments that might affect them—to continually survey and monitor the reality "out there" as well as inside the organization. This is especially true during the planning process. Five separate but overlapping environments, in particular, should be monitored (see Figure 5): the macro environment (e.g., economic trends, inflation, changes in consumer needs, even wars), the industry environment (especially trends), the competitive environment (what is the present and potential competition? how strong is it?), the customer environment (what does the customer say?), and the organization's internal environment (e.g., is there antiquated machinery? high turnover? are many people planning to retire soon?). These areas should be surveyed in depth to contribute to planning to plan, to the values audit, to the strategic business model, and to the other phases of the process. Environmental scanning also will *identify* a variety of factors, both internal and external to the organization, to be considered as part of the strategic planning process. In fact, one of the extra benefits of strategic planning is that your organization will gain a better understanding of how environmental scanning should be done.

Factors to be considered as part of the macro-environmental-scanning process include social factors such as demographics, technological factors such as the large-scale use of microcomputers, economic factors such as interest rates, and political factors such as increasing governmental deregulation. Among the factors to be considered as part of the industry environment are the structure of the industry, how the industry is financed, the degree of governmental presence, the typical products used in the industry, and the typical marketing strategies of the industry. The competitive-environment scan includes consideration of general competitor profiles, market-segmentation patterns, research and development, and so on. A great deal can be learned from the customer environment if attention is paid to returned items; complaints, compliments, and other opinions of customers; and patterns of buying. Finally, among the factors to be considered as part of the internal organizational environment are the structure of your organization, its history, and its distinctive strengths and weaknesses. Predicting how each of these areas might affect the organization over time is an essential part of the strategic planning process, one that needs to be considered in each phase. Environmental scanning is not a *phase* of the strategic planning process; it is an ongoing function of the organization that becomes especially critical during the many phases of the strategic planning process.

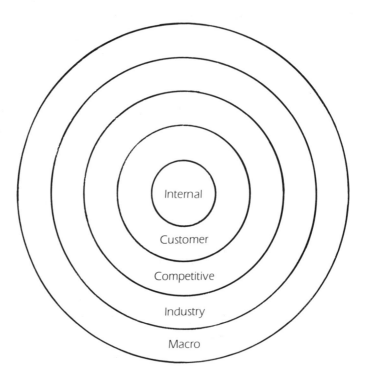

Figure 5. Environments To Be Monitored

Conclusion

Organizations need strategic planning because the world changes constantly. It is foolhardy and unrealistic to assume that economic conditions, consumer needs and expectations, competition in the marketplace, or a host of other factors will be the same two, three, or five years from now as they are today. The strategic planning process is a systematic effort by your organization to deal with the inevitability of change and to attempt to envision its own future. The importance of this process is that it enables the organization to help to *shape* its own future rather than to simply *prepare* for the future.

The Applied Strategic Planning Model presented in this booklet is markedly different from others, in both content and in process. The differences lie primarily in the attention paid to the psychological aspects of the process, especially during the values audit; in the importance of the mission formulation; and in the emphasis on proactive futuring in the development of the strategic business model. This model also is more process oriented than the others now found in the literature. It pays more attention to how the planning process works and less attention to the plan that the process generates. It also is specifically sequenced, with each phase of the process building on the preceding ones. Finally, the involvement of managers and other key members of the organization, the examination of the social and psychological underpinnings of the organization, the constant environmental surveillance, and the ongoing awareness of the need for implementation throughout the planning process produce a broader and yet more detailed, more immediately applicable plan than that which results from using other models. This truly is Applied Strategic Planning, an activity that can provide you with criteria for making important day-to-day decisions in your organization.

References

Deal, T.E., & Kennedy, A.A. *Corporate cultures: The rites and rituals of corporate life.* Reading, MA: Addison-Wesley, 1982.

Goodstein, L.D., Pfeiffer, J.W., & Nolan, T.M. Applied strategic planning: A new model for organizational growth and vitality. In L.D. Goodstein & J.W. Pfeiffer (Eds.), *The 1985 annual: Developing human resources.* San Diego, CA: University Associates, 1985.

Levitt, T. Marketing myopia. *Harvard Business Review,* September-October, 1975, pp. 26-28, 33-34, 38-39, 44, 173-174, 176-181.

Peters, T.J., & Waterman, R.H. *In search of excellence: Lessons from America's best-run companies*. New York: Harper & Row, 1982.

Pfeiffer, J.W., Goodstein, L.D., & Nolan, T.M. *Applied strategic planning: A how to do it guide*. San Diego, CA: University Associates, 1986.

Rokeach, M. *The nature of human values*. New York: Free Press, 1973.

Steiner, G.A. *Strategic planning: What every manager should know*. New York: Free Press, 1979.

Tregoe, B.B., & Zimmerman, J.W. *Top management strategy: What it is and how to make it work*. New York: Simon & Schuster, 1980.